AF375270

Numbers 1 to 100

(Forward Counting)

1	11	21	31	41	51	61	71	81	91
2	12	22	32	42	52	62	72	82	92
3	13	23	33	43	53	63	73	83	93
4	14	24	34	44	54	64	74	84	94
5	15	25	35	45	55	65	75	85	95
6	16	26	36	46	56	66	76	86	96
7	17	27	37	47	57	67	77	87	97
8	18	28	38	48	58	68	78	88	98
9	19	29	39	49	59	69	79	89	99
10	20	30	40	50	60	70	80	90	100

Practice Writing Numbers 1 - 20

Date:_______

Practice Writing Numbers 1 - 10 Date:_______

Classwork

Home Assignment

Practice Writing Numbers 1 - 10 Date:_______

Classwork

Home Assignment

Practice Writing Numbers

Classwork   Home Assignment

Fill in the blanks with missing number.

Classwork

1 __ 3 __
5 __ 7 8
7 __ 9 __
2 __ __ 5
4 __ 6 __

Home Assignment

1 2 __ __
5 __ 7 __
6 7 __ 9
3 __ __ 6
7 __ __ 10

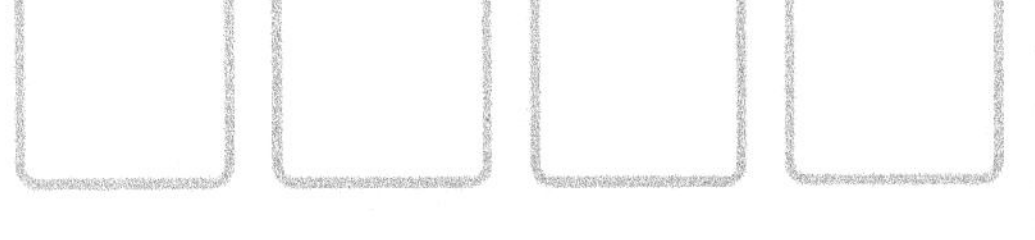

Practice Writing Numbers

Classwork   **Home Assignment**

Fill in the blanks with the number
which comes in between the given numbers in each set.

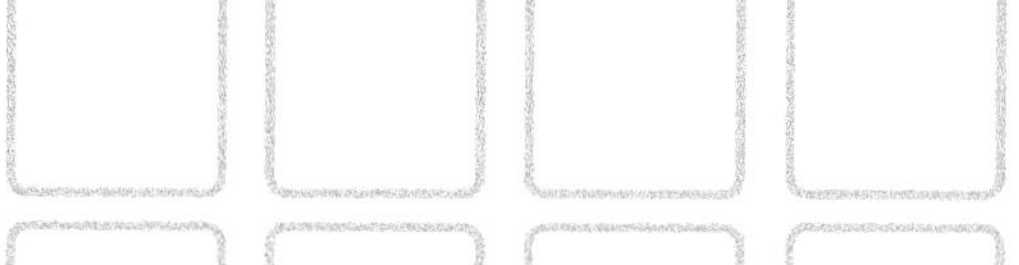

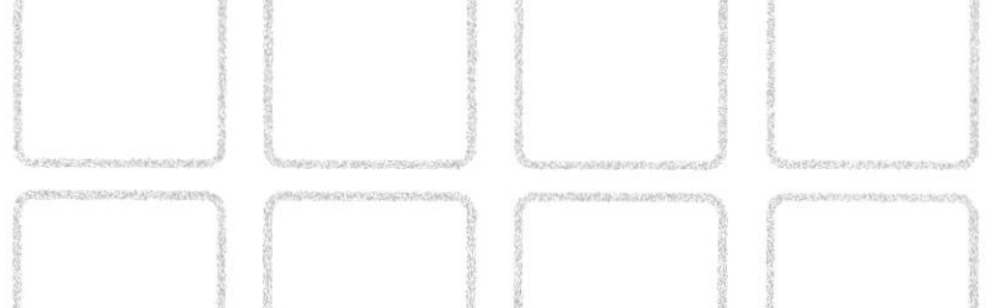

Classwork

1 __ 3

3 __ 5

6 __ 8

7 __ 9

9 __ 11

Home Assignment

2 __ 4

5 __ 7

8 __ 10

4 __ 6

1 __ 3

Practice Writing Numbers

Classwork   **Home Assignment**

Fill in the blanks with the number
which comes after the given number in each set.

Classwork

2 __	10 __
9 __	3 __
7 __	6 __
5 __	8 __
4 __	1 __

Home Assignment

3 __	6 __
10 __	2 __
5 __	1 __
9 __	8 __
7 __	4 __

Practice Writing Numbers 11 - 20

Classwork

Home Assignment

Practice Writing Numbers 11 - 20

Date:_______

Classwork

Home Assignment

Practice Writing Numbers

Date:_______

Classwork   Home Assignment

Fill in the blanks with missing number.

Classwork

1	__	3	__
12	__	14	15
16	__	18	__
9	__	__	12
17	__	19	__

Home Assignment

8	9	__	__
14	__	16	__
18	19	__	21
15	__	__	18
12	__	__	15

Practice Writing Numbers

Classwork   Home Assignment

Fill in the blanks with the number
which comes in between the given numbers in each set.

Classwork

12 __ 14

16 __ 18

19 __ 21

8 __ 10

9 __ 11

Home Assignment

18 __ 20

7 __ 9

17 __ 19

14 __ 16

10 __ 12

Practice Writing Numbers

Classwork **Home Assignment**

Fill in the blanks with the number which comes after the given number in each set.

Classwork

12 __	20 __
19 __	13 __
9 __	16 __
15 __	18 __
14 __	11 __

Home Assignment

2 __	6 __
10 __	12 __
3 __	5 __
9 __	8 __
17 __	4 __

Practice Writing Numbers 21 - 30

Classwork

Home Assignment

Practice Writing Numbers 21 - 30

Date:______

Classwork

Home Assignment

Practice Writing Numbers

Classwork	Home Assignment

Fill in the blanks with missing number.

Classwork

21	__	23	--
22	__	24	25
27	__	29	__
19	__	__	22
9	__	11	__

Home Assignment

27	28	__	--
24	__	26	--
19	20	__	22
25	__	__	28
22	__	__	25

Practice Writing Numbers

Classwork	Home Assignment

Fill in the blanks with the number which comes in between the given numbers in each set.

Classwork

25 __ 27

22 __ 24

26 __ 28

29 __ 31

19 __ 21

Home Assignment

21 __ 23

24 __ 26

27 __ 29

25 __ 27

29 __ 31

Practice Writing Numbers

Classwork   Home Assignment

Fill in the blanks with the number which comes after the given number in each set.

Classwork

22 __   20 __

29 __   13 __

27 __   23 __

25 __   28 __

24 __   21 __

Home Assignment

13 __   16 __

9 __   22 __

25 __   21 __

19 __   18 __

26 __   14 __

Practice Writing Numbers 31 - 40

Date:_______

Classwork   **Home Assignment**

Practice Writing Numbers 31 - 40

Date:_______

Classwork

Home Assignment

Practice Writing Numbers

Classwork	Home Assignment

Fill in the blanks with missing number.

Classwork

31 __ 33 __

22 __ 24 25

33 __ 35 __

29 __ __ 32

35 __ 37 __

Home Assignment

28 29 __ __

34 __ 36 __

35 36 __ 38

25 __ __ 28

29 __ __ 32

Practice Writing Numbers

Classwork **Home Assignment**

Fill in the blanks with the number which comes in between the given numbers in each set.

Classwork

32 __ 34

36 __ 38

35 __ 37

29 __ 31

38 __ 40

Home Assignment

28 __ 30

31 __ 33

36 __ 38

24 __ 26

30 __ 32

Practice Writing Numbers

Classwork   Home Assignment

Fill in the blanks with the number which comes after the given number in each set.

Classwork

32	__	40	__
39	__	36	__
37	__	19	__
35	__	28	__
34	__	20	__

Home Assignment

33	__	16	__
39	__	22	__
29	__	31	__
19	__	30	__
28	__	38	__

Practice Writing Numbers 41 - 50

Date:________

Classwork

Home Assignment

Practice Writing Numbers 41 - 50

Date:_______

Classwork

Home Assignment

Date:_______

Classwork   Home Assignment

Fill in the blanks with missing number.

Classwork

41	__	43	__
42	__	44	45
46	__	48	__
39	__	__	42
47	__	49	__

Home Assignment

38	39	__	__
44	__	46	__
48	49	__	51
35	__	__	38
39	__	__	42

Practice Writing Numbers

Classwork   Home Assignment

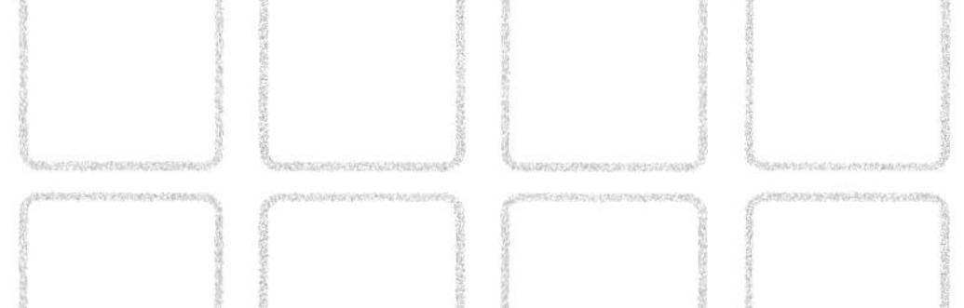

Fill in the blanks with the number which comes in between the given numbers in each set.

Classwork

42 __ 44

36 __ 38

49 __ 51

48 __ 50

39 __ 41

Home Assignment

43 __ 45

47 __ 49

38 __ 40

29 __ 31

45 __ 47

Practice Writing Numbers

Classwork **Home Assignment**

Fill in the blanks with the number
which comes after the given number in each set.

Classwork

42 __	40 __
49 __	34 __
47 __	45 __
41 __	48 __
36 __	31 __

Home Assignment

43 __	46 __
33 __	40 __
39 __	31 __
29 __	19 __
37 __	44 __

Practice Writing Numbers 51 - 60

Classwork

Home Assignment

Practice Writing Numbers 51 - 60

Date:_______

Classwork

Home Assignment

Practice Writing Numbers

Classwork	Home Assignment

Fill in the blanks with missing number.

Classwork

49	__	51	__
53	__	55	56
56	__	58	__
52	__	__	55
39	__	41	__

Home Assignment

48	49	__	__
50	__	52	__
54	55	__	57
57	__	__	60
32	__	__	35

Practice Writing Numbers

Classwork   **Home Assignment**

Fill in the blanks with the number
which comes in between the given number in each set.

Classwork

52 __ 54

56 __ 58

29 __ 31

42 __ 44

55 __ 57

Home Assignment

42 __ 44

27 __ 29

54 __ 56

53 __ 55

58 __ 60

Practice Writing Numbers

Classwork   **Home Assignment**

Fill in the blanks with the number
which comes after the given number in each set.

Classwork

52 __		10 __
59 __		23 __
37 __		56 __
55 __		58 __
44 __		51 __

Home Assignment

53 __		46 __
50 __		22 __
47 __		31 __
29 __		50 __
57 __		54 __

Practice Writing Numbers 61 - 70

Classwork

Home Assignment

Practice Writing Numbers 61 - 70

Classwork

Home Assignment

Practice Writing Numbers

Classwork **Home Assignment**

Fill in the blanks with missing number.

Classwork

60 __ 62 __
64 __ 66 67
56 __ 58 __
59 __ __ 62
63 __ 65 __

Home Assignment

67 68 __ __
64 __ 66 __
58 59 __ __
25 __ __ 28
49 __ __ 52

Practice Writing Numbers

Classwork   **Home Assignment**

Fill in the blanks with the number which comes in between the given number in each set.

Classwork

62 __ 64

66 __ 68

59 __ 61

48 __ 50

32 __ 34

Home Assignment

68 __ 70

52 __ 54

67 __ 69

44 __ 46

23 __ 25

Practice Writing Numbers

Classwork Home Assignment

Fill in the blanks with the number which comes after the given number in each set.

Classwork

69 __	50 __
29 __	60 __
67 __	56 __
45 __	19 __
64 __	61 __

Home Assignment

63 __	46 __
10 __	62 __
65 __	51 __
68 __	38 __
57 __	66 __

Practice Writing Numbers 71 - 80

Date:_______

Classwork

Home Assignment

Classwork

Home Assignment

Practice Writing Numbers

Classwork	Home Assignment

Fill in the blanks with missing number.

Classwork

69	__	71	__
72	__	74	75
66	__	68	__
76	__	__	79
57	__	59	__

Home Assignment

68	69	__	__
74	__	76	__
58	59	__	61
75	__	__	78
69	__	__	72

Practice Writing Numbers

Classwork **Home Assignment**

**Fill in the blanks with the number
which comes in between the given number in each set.**

Classwork

72 __ 74

78 __ 80

29 __ 31

56 __ 58

44 __ 46

Home Assignment

73 __ 75

77 __ 79

70 __ 72

64 __ 66

59 __ 61

Practice Writing Numbers

Classwork **Home Assignment**

Fill in the blanks with the number
which comes after the given number in each set.

Classwork

79	__	60	__
39	__	53	__
77	__	16	__
65	__	79	__
74	__	71	__

Home Assignment

73	__	59	__
10	__	72	__
75	__	80	__
52	__	76	__
78	__	34	__

Practice Writing Numbers 81 - 90

Date:_______

Classwork

Home Assignment

Practice Writing Numbers 81 - 90

Date:_______

Classwork

Home Assignment

Date:_______

Classwork   Home Assignment

Fill in the blanks with missing number

Classwork

81 __ 83 __

85 __ 87 88

84 __ 86 __

59 __ __ 62

46 __ 48 __

Home Assignment

78 79 __ __

34 __ 36 __

58 59 __ 61

65 __ __ 68

42 __ __ 45

Practice Writing Numbers

Classwork		Home Assignment	

Fill in the blanks with the number which comes in between the given number in each set.

Classwork

89 __ 91

67 __ 69

85 __ 87

42 __ 44

31 __ 33

Home Assignment

56 __ 58

27 __ 29

43 __ 45

89 __ 91

79 __ 81

Practice Writing Numbers

Classwork   Home Assignment

Fill in the blanks with the number which comes after the given number in each set.

Classwork

88	__	80	__
89	__	37	__
77	__	86	__
63	__	79	__
19	__	84	__

Home Assignment

83	__	61	__
10	__	82	__
85	__	86	__
69	__	81	__
72	__	74	__

Practice Writing Numbers 91 - 100

Date:_______

Classwork

Home Assignment

Practice Writing Numbers 91 - 100

Date:_______

Classwork

Home Assignment

Practice Writing Numbers

Classwork

Home Assignment

Fill in the blanks with missing number.

Classwork

89	__	91	__
94	__	96	97
92	__	94	__
87	__	__	90
69	__	71	__

Home Assignment

96	97	__	__
92	__	94	__
81	82	__	84
55	__	__	58
79	__	__	82

Practice Writing Numbers

Classwork   Home Assignment

Fill in the blanks with the number

Classwork

89 __ __

9 __ __

19 __ __

79 __ __

99 __ __

Home Assignment

39 __ __

59 __ __

69 __ __

29 __ __

49 __ __

Date:_______

Classwork   **Home Assignment**

Fill in the blanks with the number
which comes after the given number in each set.

Classwork

99 __	92 __
87 __	79 __
89 __	93 __
95 __	96 __
91 __	80 __

Home Assignment

83 __	66 __
70 __	94 __
77 __	90 __
42 __	78 __
63 __	72 __

Write the numbers which come after given number

Classwork	Home Assignment

Classwork

29 __ __

59 __ __

89 __ __

69 __ __

9 __ __

49 __ __

79 __ __

39 __ __

19 __ __

99 __ __

Home Assignment

38 __ __ __

28 __ __ __

18 __ __ __

68 __ __ __

88 __ __ __

78 __ __ __

48 __ __ __

8 __ __ __

58 __ __ __

98 __ __ __

Numbers 100 to 1

(Backward Counting)

100	90	80	70	60	50	40	30	20	10
99	89	79	69	59	49	39	29	19	9
98	88	78	68	58	48	38	28	18	8
97	87	77	67	57	47	37	27	17	7
96	86	76	66	56	46	36	26	16	6
95	85	75	65	55	45	35	25	15	5
94	84	74	64	54	44	34	24	14	4
93	83	73	63	53	43	33	23	13	3
92	82	72	62	52	42	32	22	12	2
91	81	71	61	51	41	31	21	11	1

Date:_______

1 to 20 Forward

20 - 1 Backwards

Practice Writing Numbers

Classwork   **Home Assignment**

Fill in the blanks with the number
which comes before the given number in each set.

Classwork

__ 12   __ 11
__ 8   __ 10
__ 19   __ 3
__ 15   __ 7
__ 14   __ 16

Home Assignment

__ 5   __ 2
__ 18   __ 17
__ 9   __ 6
__ 8   __ 20
__ 13   __ 4

Practice Writing Numbers Backwards 20 - 1

Date:_________

Classwork   **Home Assignment**

Practice Writing Numbers Backwards 20 - 1

Date:_______

Classwork

Home Assignment

Practice Writing Numbers Backwards 20 - 1

Date:________

Classwork

Home Assignment

Write the number which comes after given number

87 __   9 __

34 __   66 __

22 __   42 __

Write the number which comes in between the given numbers

56 __ 58   __ 90 __

69 __ 71   __ 40 __

29 __ 31   __ 20 __

Write the number which comes before given number

__ 11   __ 18

__ 7   __ 15

__ 10   __ 13

Practice Writing Numbers Backwards 40 - 20

Date:_______

20 - 40 Forward

40 - 20 Backwards

Practice Writing Numbers

Classwork   **Home Assignment**

Fill in the blanks with the number
which comes before the given number in each set.

Classwork

__ 39   __ 31
__ 23   __ 38
__ 29   __ 34
__ 35   __ 40
__ 24   __ 26

Home Assignment

__ 5   __ 32
__ 28   __ 37
__ 19   __ 16
__ 36   __ 30
__ 33   __ 40

Practice Writing Numbers Backwards 40 - 20

Date:_______

Classwork

Home Assignment

Complete the backward number counting - Classwork

40   --   --   --   --   --   --

32   --   --   --   --   --   --

12   --   --   --   --   --   --

9   --   --   --   --   --   --

25   --   --   --   --   --   --

Home Assignment

23   --   --   --   --   --   --

38   --   --   --   --   --   --

8   --   --   --   --   --   --

27   --   --   --   --   --   --

31   --   --   --   --   --   --

19   --   --   --   --   --   --

Practice Writing Numbers Backwards 40 - 20

Date:________

Classwork

Home Assignment

Write the number which comes after given number

98 __   59 __

56 __   42 __

71 __   29 __

Write the number which comes in between the given numbers

41 __ 43   __ 10 __

66 __ 68   __ 30 __

32 __ 34   __ 60 __

Write the number which comes before given number

__ 28   __ 21

__ 31   __ 30

__ 20   __ 35

Date:________

40 - 60 Forward

60 - 40 Backwards

Practice Writing Numbers

Classwork   Home Assignment

Fill in the blanks with the number
which comes before the given number in each set.

Classwork

__	42	__	11
__	58	__	50
__	49	__	53
__	45	__	57
__	54	__	60

Home Assignment

__	35	__	52
__	48	__	47
__	59	__	56
__	46	__	40
__	23	__	44

Date:_______

Classwork

Home Assignment

Complete the backward number counting - Classwork

60 __ __ __ __ __ __

52 __ __ __ __ __ __

47 __ __ __ __ __ __

32 __ __ __ __ __ __

25 __ __ __ __ __ __

Home Assignment

51 __ __ __ __ __ __

22 __ __ __ __ __ __

46 __ __ __ __ __ __

34 __ __ __ __ __ __

13 __ __ __ __ __ __

9 __ __ __ __ __ __

Practice Writing Numbers Backwards 60 - 40

Date:________

Classwork

Home Assignment

Write the number which comes after given number

89 __   40 __

69 __   57 __

35 __   23 __

Write the number which comes in between the given numbers

19 __ 21   __ 80 __

52 __ 54   __ 30 __

70 __ 72   __ 50 __

Write the number which comes before given number

__ 70   __ 40

__ 55   __ 60

__ 51   __ 41

Practice Writing Numbers Backwards 80 - 60

Date:_______

60 - 80 Forward

80 - 60 Backwards

Practice Writing Numbers

Classwork   Home Assignment

Fill in the blanks with the number which comes before the given number in each set.

Classwork

__	72	__	71
__	68	__	80
__	79	__	63
__	65	__	77
__	14	__	66

Home Assignment

__	75	__	62
__	78	__	67
__	69	__	65
__	76	__	70
__	73	__	64

Practice Writing Numbers Backwards 80 - 60

Date:_______

Classwork

Home Assignment

Complete the backward number counting - Classwork

72   __   __   __   __   __   __

80   __   __   __   __   __   __

63   __   __   __   __   __   __

52   __   __   __   __   __   __

46   __   __   __   __   __   __

Home Assignment

83   __   __   __   __   __   __

27   __   __   __   __   __   __

56   __   __   __   __   __   __

32   __   __   __   __   __   __

17   __   __   __   __   __   __

48   __   __   __   __   __   __

Practice Writing Numbers Backwards 80 - 60

Classwork

Home Assignment

Write the number which comes after given number

9 __   32 __

28 __   50 __

48 __   17 __

Write the number which comes in between the given numbers

59 __ 61   __ 16 __

72 __ 74   __ 99 __

89 __ 91   __ 70 __

Write the number which comes before given number

__ 80   __ 61

__ 78   __ 70

__ 71   __ 60

Practice Writing Numbers Backwards 100 - 80

Date:_______

80 - 100 Forward

100 - 80 Backwards

Practice Writing Numbers

Classwork   Home Assignment

Fill in the blanks with the number which comes before the given number in each set.

Classwork

__	97	__	93
__	89	__	85
__	90	__	83
__	96	__	87
__	53	__	92

Home Assignment

__	65	__	81
__	89	__	50
__	40	__	82
__	91	__	71
__	90	__	98

Practice Writing Numbers Backwards 100 - 80   Date:_______

Classwork

Home Assignment

Complete the backward number counting - Classwork

82 __ __ __ __ __ __

91 __ __ __ __ __ __

67 __ __ __ __ __ __

100 __ __ __ __ __ __

89 __ __ __ __ __ __

Home Assignment

100 __ __ __ __ __ __

95 __ __ __ __ __ __

86 __ __ __ __ __ __

72 __ __ __ __ __ __

65 __ __ __ __ __ __

53 __ __ __ __ __ __

Practice Writing Numbers Backwards 100 - 80

Date:________

Classwork

Home Assignment

Write the number which comes after given number

79 __   19 __

82 __   80 __

92 __   43 __

Write the number which comes in between the given numbers

69 __ 71   __ 40 __

89 __ 91   __ 20 __

34 __ 36   __ 50 __

Write the number which comes before given number

__ 40   __ 50

__ 20   __ 80

__ 90   __ 100

Write the numbers which comes before given number

Classwork		Home Assignment		
31 __ __		32 __ __ __		
51 __ __		22 __ __ __		
81 __ __		62 __ __ __		
61 __ __		82 __ __ __		
11 __ __		42 __ __ __		
41 __ __		99 __ __ __		
71 __ __		12 __ __ __		
91 __ __		52 __ __ __		
21 __ __		72 __ __ __		
100 __ __		92 __ __ __		

Date:_______

Write the number which comes after the given number

79 __   19 __

82 __   80 __

92 __   43 __

Fill in the missing numbers.

69 __ 71   __ 40 __

89 __ 91   __ 20 __

34 __ 36   __ 50 __

Write the number which comes before the given number

__ 40   __ 50

__ 20   __ 80

__ 90   __ 100

Write the numbers which comes before the given number

31 __ __	32 __ __ __
51 __ __	22 __ __ __
81 __ __	62 __ __ __
61 __ __	82 __ __ __
11 __ __	42 __ __ __
41 __ __	99 __ __ __
71 __ __	12 __ __ __
91 __ __	52 __ __ __
21 __ __	72 __ __ __
100 __ __	92 __ __ __